The Seed of the Word

Katherine D. Walker

ISBN 979-8-89526-574-1 (paperback)
ISBN 979-8-89526-575-8 (digital)

Christian Faith Publishing
832 Park Avenue
Meadville, PA 16335
www.christianfaithpublishing.com

Printed in the United States of America

CONTENTS

Blessings to all.

I have not stopped praying for you. I continually ask God to fill you with the knowledge of his will through all the wisdom and understanding that the Spirit gives so that you may live a life worthy of the LORD and please him in every way: bearing fruit in every good work, growing in the knowledge of God, being strengthened with all power according to his glorious might so that you may have great endurance and patience, and giving joyful thanks to the Father, who has qualified you to share in the inheritance of his holy people in the kingdom of light (Colossians 1:9–12).

KATHERINE'S STORY

The moment that I accepted Jesus as my Savior (at the age of eight), he wrapped me in his liquid love that changed my life forever. From that time on, I started having loving encounters with my Jesus. There was a church located down the hill and across the street from my home. The back of the church faced the right side of my home. There was a section of trees at the back right side of the church. Whenever I would walk to that side, I would always look back home. In a sense, it was as if I could just get to the church; I could see my way home. That statement became resoundingly true as I matured.

On the side of that church was my special place with my Jesus. On many occasions, Jesus would step into the gentle breeze as it blew through the trees. He wasn't always in the breeze, but when Jesus would show up, he would wrap me in liquid love. I would close my eyes with my hands spread apart as if I would hug Jesus. I twirled around, laughed, and danced with him. Although I didn't see his face during those times, I could feel him and hear him tell me when it was time to go home.

As I grew, my love and hunger to know more about Jesus increased. During my teenage years, I was so on fire for my LORD. Unfortunately, during a frustrating season, I rebelled against the One I loved. The Holy One took me through a series of course corrections. I didn't understand the battles that I was having until Jesus lovingly revealed to me that I had not made him LORD of my life. When Jesus became not only my Savior but now my LORD, at that very moment, I began to truly live.

Then life happened a few years later that caused a spirit of heaviness to rest upon me, which turned into a very deep depression. I was strongly considering ending my life. I remember calling on Jesus and asking him to save me and then crying myself to sleep. After I felt myself drifting off to sleep immediately, my room was filled with the brightest white light that had never been seen on earth. As I turned over onto my left side, I was face-to-face with Jesus!

He had no smile nor a frown on his face. Jesus had a look of concern, and his eyes were full of love. There was a three- to five-inch blue aura around his head. His love was so intense that I was in the fetal position, and my body shook uncontrollably from the love that flowed through me. Because of the glory flowing through his face, I could barely look at him. My spirit craved more of him, but my body could not handle much more. I was healed from depression instantly. Throughout my journey, I have had many more encounters with Jesus. I am just a lowly and humble servant who is to proclaim what I have seen, experienced, and know to his church. The anointing is upon everyone who believes in Jesus, but walking in the fullness of it will cost you all.

INTRODUCTION

The Seed of the Word is a prophetic utterance from the heart of the Almighty. There is an urgency from the Almighty Father for his children to come up higher as we enter the secret place of the Most High. We are seated with Christ Jesus in heavenly places, and from this vantage point, we will receive strategies to war against what's coming.

Let the "remnant" arise! This is not the time to get out the "rapture rug." This is the greatest time ever to be alive. This book will give insight into what is coming, how to stay in a submitted position, drive back the darkness, align in total surrender to the Holy Spirit, and through his guidance, how to build, war, and empower the next generation. The Spirit of Truth knows the heart of the Almighty. We will be trained on how to walk in sonship, operate in our kingly authority, and do great exploits to further the kingdom of God in Jesus's name.

CHAPTER 1

The Oldest Covenant

> He remembers his covenant forever, the promise he made, for a thousand generations. (Psalms 105:8 NIV)

What is a covenant? A formal, solemn, and binding agreement: compact…international law, which depends upon the sanctity of agreements between rulers. A formal alliance or agreement made by God with a people or with humanity in general.

God is one but exists in three persons (Father, Son, and Spirit) who made an agreement to make man in his image and likeness. Mankind is the only created being that possesses divine blood. The Almighty made a mold of himself and breathed eternity into the nostrils of Adam, who became a living soul. The light of eternity is the life of all mankind. We were created to carry and release the glory of the Most High God.

We have been given a glimpse of how the first Adam looked before sin when we read Luke 9:28–36. In this account, we see Jesus (who is the last Adam) go up to a mountain to pray and transform before Peter, James, and John. Jesus reveals his glorious divinity to these disciples as they beheld the glory of the only begotten Son of God. The divine blood that flowed through the first Adam became contaminated by sin, but through the last Adam (Jesus), it became mankind's redemption.

In him was life, and the life was the light of men.
The light shines in the darkness and the darkness
did not comprehend it (John 1:4–5 NASB).

Before the fall, the LORD God would visit with mankind (male and female) in the cool of the day not only to commune with them but to instruct them in how the kingdom of God operated. These word-based principles were to be duplicated and carried out to govern the earth's realm. The Word of God cultivated the earth in such a way that mankind lacked nothing. The four great rivers were used as markers to pinpoint the locations of gold, bdellium (a fragrant resin like myrrh), and onyx stones that were found in the lands near them. The LORD God went on to explain the principle of seedtime and harvest before establishing the divine covenant with Adam.

The test of obedience was declared to Adam by the LORD. The LORD God gave him instructions about the tree of the knowledge of good and evil. This was God's divine portion, or as we now know, the tithe, which is holy to the LORD. When the appointed time was to come, Adam was to offer up the fruit to the LORD God. If mankind had obeyed God's command, then all the other trees would have been sanctified, and their fruits would have been increased by the Word of the LORD God.

And the LORD God commanded the man, "You
are free to eat from any tree in the garden; but
you must not eat from the tree of the knowledge
of good and evil, for when you eat from it you
will certainly die." (Genesis 2:16–17 NIV)

Tithing Covenant

And he remembered for them his covenant and
repented according to the multitude of his mercies. (Psalm 106:45 KJV)

Tithing is the oldest covenant that was established by God. Tithing is a spiritual principle that originated from God. It (tithing) was a means by which God used to sanctify the rest of the harvest. Once the harvest was sanctified, the "first fruits" would be considered holy to God when they were presented by mankind. Once the covenant was established, then God put man to sleep and created woman. The woman or *(wombed man)* was to be a helpmate to rule with the same authority on the earth as the man. They would operate in unity as one flesh. The man was to instruct the woman as he was instructed by God concerning the covenant.

In the garden, the woman was deceived by the serpent to *eat God's divine seed. The tithe is also a divine seed of God.* Adam willingly rebelled and ate the divine seed of God (*the tree of the knowledge of good and evil*). Before the woman was created, Adam was told that if he obeyed the voice of God, it would produce an eternal harvest. However, if he chooses to transgress the command of God, it will bring about the curse of death. Throughout the generations, the serpent of old, who is Satan, has convinced many of God's children to continue to eat the divine seed in the form of the tithe.

> But like Adam they have transgressed the covenant; There they have dealt treacherously against Me. (Hosea 6:7 NASB)

This sacred covenant of the tithe has been misunderstood by many. Due to corruption and ignorance of others, this holy covenant has been deemed a by-product of man's greed. Everything that is established by the Almighty, the evil one, always tries to pervert. Through man's oral traditions of passing information down from generation to generation, some inconsistencies happened.

In other words, trusting in the world's system will cause those who depend on it to stay impoverished and always in debt. *Debt is a curse.* When we align with the principles of "the kingdom of God," the Father promises to give us the power to obtain wealth (Deuteronomy 8:18). This power is spiritual, physical, and financial. There is no lack in the kingdom of God. The sanctification process begins within our hearts and is a constant reminder of who has blessed us…our God.

> Thus says the LORD, "Cursed is the man who trusts in mankind and makes flesh his strength, and whose heart turns away from the LORD. For he will be like a bush in the desert and will not see when prosperity comes, but will live in stony wastes in the wilderness, a land of salt without inhabitant." (Jeremiah 17:5–6)

Seedtime and Harvest

Seedtime and harvest are the spiritual principles behind tithing, and it is how the kingdom of God operates. Adam created as God did with the words of his mouth. Because of the righteousness of God, which flowed through mankind, immediate manifestations occurred. These righteous words of mankind would eventually produce a tangible harvest. Mankind would simply speak to what God had created, and it would produce. The sons and daughters of God were created to rule with him by using this principle. The earth is the LORD's and all it contains.

Mankind regularly sows words that lead to actions every day. If our words are of wickedness and rebellion, then we can expect to reap destruction and death. If our words sown are aligned with the Word of God, which is righteousness and truth, then we can expect to reap salvation and life. There are angels who were created to reap mankind's harvest. These angels of God collect the harvest of the saints from righteous words and deeds and present it to the LORD God. Those who have chosen to live in darkness have fallen angels to present the harvest of rebellion that leads to destruction.

> As long as the earth endures, seedtimes and harvest, cold and heat, summer and winter, day and night will never cease. (Genesis 8:22 NIV)

CHAPTER 2

Marriage Covenant

And the LORD God fashioned into a woman the rib which He had taken from the man and brought her to the man. Then the man said, "At last this is bone of my bones, and flesh of my flesh; she shall be called woman, because she was taken out of man." For this reason, a man shall leave his father and his mother, and be joined to his wife; and they shall become one flesh. (Genesis 2:22–24 NASB)

The marriage covenant is a sacred union that was established by God. Mankind was created to produce through this state of unity. As the three persons of the Godhead (Father, Son, and Spirit) are one, mankind was to mirror a similar relationship. The man was created to carry the seed, but the woman (or wombed man) was created to produce the fruit of the seed.

In the beginning, the Almighty never intended for the woman to be subservient to the man. In fact, *Genesis 2:18* describes the woman as a suitable helper for Adam. The word "helpmate" in Hebrew is "Ezer Kenegdo." "Ezer" means to rescue or save, to strongly support. While "Kenegdo" means equally and uniquely created, fitting together perfectly. The phrase "helpmate" establishes the woman as a partner with Adam and not to be positioned in an inferior role to him.

In a sense, through the sovereignty of God, who pulled the fruit out of the seed of man and formed woman. This woman was the fruit of mankind who was created to produce fruit from the womb. Thus, God ordained that man could not produce alone, but through unity, multiplication is birthed. This is a spiritual principle that also manifests in the natural realm.

In ancient Israel, the betrothal and marriage process were a picture of God's redemption plan for mankind. In ancient times, a father would acquire a wife for his son within the family clan or tribe. A perfect picture of this is when Abraham sent his servant to Sarah's relatives to get a wife for his son Isaac.

The servant prayed to the God of Abraham for favor and success in his mission. As the servant completed his prayer, Rebecca came to the well to draw water. After Rebecca fulfilled the signs that the servant asked God for, he then gave her a *mattan* (*a gift*) in the form of a gold ring and two gold bracelets. Upon Rebecca agreeing to leave with the servant to become Isaac's wife, the servant gave "precious things" to Laban (her brother) and her mother a *mohar* (purchase price).

> Isaac brought her into the tent of his mother Sarah, and he married Rebekah. So, she became his wife, and he loved her; and Isaac was comforted after his mother's death. (Genesis 24:67 NIV)

In ancient times, marriage consisted of two ceremonies that were officiated at two separate times. First was the *betrothal* (in Hebrew: *erusin*) and later, the *wedding* (in Hebrew: *nissuin*). There was an interval of time between the betrothal and the wedding. Another biblical example of this is Joseph and Mary (the parents of Jesus).

A woman was deemed to be legally married at the time of betrothal, although she still lived with her parents. Once the day of the wedding came, *the betrothed woman would be accompanied by a procession from her parent's home to the groom's home. (This is a picture of the rapture of the "church").* Marriage was made legal after the consummation. The *shedding of blood* at the time of consummation was *a sign of purity* in the bride.

How is marriage a picture of the Almighty's redemption plan for mankind, you may ask? Through the omniscience of God, who knows the end from the beginning, he encrypted the redemption plan in the marriage covenant. Adam, being full of the Spirit, declared a prophetic utterance of the Almighty's plan. He stated, "For this reason, a man shall leave his father and his mother, and be joined to his wife; and they shall become one flesh."

The Apostle Paul declares, "This mystery is great; but I am speaking with reference to Christ and the church" (Ephesians 5:32 NASB). In the fullness of time, the last Adam (Jesus), who is the Word, was made flesh and dwelt among us.

The Almighty sent his Word to heal (restore, recover, and repair) the breach between God and mankind.

Through the sovereignty and love of the Almighty Father, he gave *Jesus as a gift* to the world, and *Jesus's shed blood was the purchase price for our sins.*

> For God so loved the world that He gave His one
> and only Son, that everyone who believes in Him
> shall not perish but have eternal life. (John 3:16)

Now to recap. Jesus left the Father's home (*heaven*) and was sent by the Father as a *gift* to mankind. The redemption or *purchase price* for our sins was the shed blood of Jesus, and the penalty of our sins was death. *Jesus died for what was killing us.* All sin was nailed to the cross through the body of Jesus. He arose from the grave and applied the shed blood (*the purchase price for sin*) to the mercy seat in heaven.

Jesus was granted permission by the Father to walk among his disciples (brothers and sisters…see 1 Corinthians 5:16) for forty days, and then he ascended back into heaven, leaving his mother (Mary) to intercede on our behalf before the Father. Thus, Jesus fulfilled the first part of the scripture: *For this reason, a man shall leave his father and his mother, and be joined to his wife; and they shall become one flesh.*

The woman who was taken out of the side of the first Adam and was stripped of her authority when she sinned. The LORD God declared, "I will greatly multiply your pain in childbirth, in pain you shall bring forth children; yet your desires shall be for your husband, and he shall rule over you" (Genesis 3:16). On the cross, *Jesus (the last Adam) reconciled the woman back to her original position of authority when his right side was pierced by the spear.*

The scriptures state that Jesus had already died when his side was pierced. To die or to sleep is the same in the sight of God. The scriptures were fulfilled through Jesus, who reconciled mankind back to the Almighty's original intention before the fall. The finished work on the cross will be upheld by the One who has completed it.

We, "the church," are betrothed to Jesus, who is coming back for his bride who has no spot or wrinkle. We are not to be like the five foolish virgins who ran out of oil waiting on the bridegroom. We are commissioned to be as the five wise virgins who carried the oil of intimacy for our Jesus.

The latter half of this scripture (*and be joined to his wife*) will be fulfilled at the return of Christ Jesus—to emphasize again that this is a picture of the rapture of the "church."

The Apostle Paul declares, "Listen, I tell you a mystery: We will not all sleep, but we will all be changed in a flash, in the twinkling of an eye, at the last trumpet. For the trumpet will sound, the dead will be raised imperishable, and we will be changed" (1 Corinthians 15:51–52).

While "the church" remains in the earthly realm, we are in the betrothal state until the appointed time set by the Father is announced. Once the fullness of time comes, we, "the church," will be ushered into the presence of God forever. For this is a trustworthy statement: *Blessed are those who are invited to the marriage supper of the Lamb (Revelation 19:9).* Upon the completion of these events, which will fulfill the prophetic utterance made by the first Adam, *for this reason, a man shall leave his father and his mother, and be joined to his wife; and they shall become one flesh.*

The Spirit and the bride say, "Come." He who has ears to hear, let him hear what the Spirit is saying to the Church.

And I will betroth you to Me forever; yes, I will betroth you to Me in righteousness and justice, in steadfast love, and in mercy. I will even betroth you to Me in stability and in faithfulness, and you shall know (recognize, be acquainted with, appreciate, give heed to, and cherish) the LORD.
(Hosea 2:19–20 AMPC)

CHAPTER 3

The First Fruit

He chose to give us birth through the word of
truth, that we might be a kind of first fruits of all
he created. (James 1:18 NIV)

Unlike tithing, which is a tenth portion of the best out of the first
portion of the harvest, a first fruit is the first of the whole of something. If mankind had not eaten the divine seed and obediently presented it, then every tree would have abundantly yielded fruit in its
season. Then the LORD Almighty would have sanctified the harvest,
and mankind could have presented a first fruit to the LORD God.

Because of the overwhelming compassion and sovereignty of
God Most High, the Lamb was slain from the foundation of the
world (Revelation 13:8). After the fall of man, the LORD God
instructed him on how to sacrifice innocent animals to make atonement for sin. God made clothing out of the skins of the animal that
was slaughtered in the place of mankind. Once man's sin was covered
by the blood of an innocent animal, then the LORD God instructed
man on how to present first fruits and also how to atone for sin.

The word atone means to make amends: to provide or serve as reparation or compensation for something bad or unwelcome.

*The word reparation means the act of making amends, offering, or
giving satisfaction for a wrong or injury.*

The first Adam and his descendants after him could only give compensation for their sins. Because mankind was now polluted with the sin nature, no one was able to make an offering that would *redeem* the weight of sin in mankind. When the fullness of time came, the last Adam *(Jesus)*, who is the Word of God, wrapped himself in flesh to redeem mankind. Until the appointed time had come, Adam was to pass down the LORD's instructions orally to his sons. As these instructions were passed down through the generations, many inconsistencies occurred. Mankind did what was right in his or her own eyes, and without the conviction of sin, mankind's practice started to morally decay. That moral decay gave birth to wickedness, and wickedness gave birth to gross perversion. Only a few held onto the teachings of the "Sons of God," who were angels clothed in flesh who instructed mankind in the ways of God. *There was no written law until the time of Moses.*

First Fruit of the Womb
The Blessing of the Firstborn Male
Oral Teaching from Adam to His Firstborn Sons

Father's Name:	Age:	Son's Name:	Father died:	Adam's Age at birth:
God	—	Adam	Eternal	
Adam	130	Seth	930	130
Seth	105	Enosh	920	235
Enosh	90	Kenan	905	325
Kenan	70	Mahalalel	910	395
Mahalalel	65	Jared	895	460
Jared	162	Enoch	962	622
Enoch	65	Methuselah	365 translated	687
Methuselah	187	Lamech	969	874
Lamech	182	Noah	777	Died 126 years before
Noah	500	Shem, Ham, Japheth	950	

> The LORD said to Moses, "Consecrate to me every firstborn male. The first offspring of every womb among the Israelites belongs to Me, whether human or animal." (Exodus 13:1–2 NIV)

The Almighty started this, and this law is still in effect because it's a spiritual principle like tithing. The heavenly Father gives all firstborn males a greater authority and favor that can affect generations. The firstborn males are born to lead, release blessings or curses, and break or add strongholds over the family. Firstborn males have great authority from the heavenly Father on earth and in heaven through the quickening of the Holy Spirit.

The evil one starts attacking mankind from conception to birth, throughout childhood, and even to adulthood. The evil one only comes to steal, kill, and destroy. *However, he can do nothing in the earth realm without the consent of mankind.* Through the illusions of power, authority, wealth, and fame that are promised by this serpent of old, many have succumbed to the subtleness of his deception. Why are firstborn males attacked more than others?

The firstborn males are seed carriers who hold the blueprints of the family and are considered holy unto the LORD. The evil one tries to take them out before they know who they are.

> For all who are being led by the Spirit of God, these are sons of God. (Romans 8:14 NASB)

In Genesis 1:26 NIV, then God said, "Let us make mankind in our image, in our likeness, so that they may rule over the fish in the sea and the birds in the sky, over the livestock and all the wild animals, and over all the creatures that move along the ground."

We were created with God's tangible frame and personality. Haven't we heard an older person say to a young child, "You are the spitting image of your dad?" They are really saying to that child, "You are the spirit image of your dad." Meaning not only does the child look like their dad, but they also behave like him.

This is what the evil one is afraid of. The devil was the anointed cherub, so he knows how powerful the anointing is. This is why he tries to destroy *all* mankind before we realize the authority we carry. Have we not read that we will judge angels (1 Corinthians 6:3)?

Many have made bad choices in life. We must realize that many of our choices were manipulated by the evil one. Many firstborn males struggle with their identity. They wrestle with how to *become who they already are.*

The tactics of the serpent of old are still the same. He tries to convince us that God is withholding something from us that we need, to twist the words or instructions given to us by God, or to cause us to question the nature or intentions of our God. The evil one is an expert in enticing our flesh with his words. In the Garden of Eden, in the wilderness with Jesus, and in our own lives, the devil entices us with our sensual desires. He is crafty in appealing to the lust of the flesh, the lust of the eyes, and the pride of life to sway us from God's will.

The only remedy to safeguard us from the enemy's attack is to saturate ourselves with *truth. Thy word oh God is truth!* We need to be washed daily with the water of the Word. This is the only weapon that Jesus, who is the Word, used to defeat the evil one in the wilderness.

We were equipped by the Almighty before we were born to shatter, destroy, and annihilate all the power of the evil one with "truth." Many of us have listened to the evil one for so long that we have started believing his lies. Our Eternal Father says that we are the apple of his eye, we are his beloved, we are more than a conqueror, we are the head, a royal priesthood, a holy nation, etc. The Father doesn't see us as a failure because we are the Spirit's image of him.

> For those God foreknew he also predestined to
> be conformed to the image of his Son, that he
> might be the firstborn among many brothers and
> sisters. (Romans 8:29 NIV)

CHAPTER 4

Like the Days of Noah

> And as it was in the days of Noah, so it will be also in the days of the Son of Man: They ate, they drank, they married wives, they were given in marriage, until the day that Noah entered the ark, and the flood came and destroyed them all. (Luke 17:26–27 NKJV)

The sin of mankind caused creation to become out of alignment with the original intentions of the LORD God. Due to the loving-kindness and compassion of the LORD God, he assigned angels, who were referred to as the "Sons of God," to teach mankind his ways. These angelic beings had flesh so that they could commune with mankind. However, once they looked upon the daughters of men and saw that they were beautiful, they transgressed the covenant assigned to them by the LORD God. This ungodly union created a *hybrid race,* which was called the *Nephilim.*

> That which is born of the flesh is flesh; and that which is born of the Spirit is spirit. (John 3:6 KJV)

This demonic breed spread throughout mankind like gangrene does in the body. These hybrid beings waxed worse and worse until a level of gross perversion and darkness blanketed mankind and all creation. This hybrid race no longer possessed the divine bloodline of the Almighty. Mankind's bloodline had become corrupted except for the lineage that the LORD God marked for his perfect will. He encrypted his redemption plan in the names of those whom he chose to be in his righteous bloodline. A divine declaration was encrypted in Adam and in his son's names revealed: the fall of mankind and the redemption of mankind through Jesus (who is the last Adam).

This declaration was based on their names: *Man is appointed mortal sorrow, but the blessed God shall come down teaching that his death shall bring the despairing rest.*

Hebrew Names	Meanings in English
Adam	Man
Seth	Appointed
Enosh	Mortal
Kenan	Sorrow
Mahalalel	The blessed God
Jared	Shall come down
Enoch	Teaching
Methuselah	His death shall bring
Lamech	The despairing
Noah	Rest

Noah would carry the imagery of this plan by the day of his birth. The scripture states that on the six hundredth year of Noah's life, on the *seventeenth day of the second month* the rain began (see Genesis 7:11–12). *The judgment of the world started on his birthday. Wow!* The second month on the Jewish calendar is the month of *Iyar.* This month falls between *May* and *June* on the modern-day/ Gregorian calendar.

According to the command of the LORD God, the animals came to Noah and entered into the ark. *The Almighty closed the door of the ark* after Noah and his family and all the animals that were marked for this salvation had entered. Any door that the Almighty closes can't be opened, nor can any doors that are opened be shut. This authority was given to mankind several centuries later and is now known as *"the key of David"* (see Isaiah 22:22 and Revelation 3:7).

God supernaturally preserved the lives of Noah and his family and the animals that were with them until the appointed time came. After over a year of being on the ark, the LORD God commanded Noah and his family, along with all the animals, to come out of the ark. They obeyed the voice of God. Later, as an act of worship, Noah presented offerings made to the LORD by fire as a pleasing aroma. This moved the heart of the *Almighty in such a way that he placed his bow in the sky.* This *rainbow* was a sign of the covenant that the LORD God made with mankind and every living creature…to never destroy the earth again with floodwaters.

So what does this have to do with this day and time? *Everything!* The LORD God reveals the end from the beginning. Preservation is in knowing and doing the will of God through his written instructions (the Bible).

The events in Genesis are paralleled in the book of Revelation. The Nephilim and the mark of the beast represent the altering of one's DNA. The Bible warns us *not* to take the mark (see Revelation 14:9–10).

Those who take the mark and worship the beast and his image will have no parts with the Almighty. These are the people who represent a heightened level of perversion in wickedness throughout mankind and gross darkness in the book of Genesis. What happened to these ones in Genesis? They all were drowned in the flood. They all received the wrath of God *for their choice* (see Revelation 14:11).

Noah and his family represent those who keep God's commands. These are the saints who live by the Word, trust, and worship the *one* true living God (see Revelation 14:12–13). As we occupy until Jesus comes, please be encouraged not to become weary in well doing, for we shall reap an eternal reward if we faint not.

Because of the increase of wickedness, the love of most will grow cold, but the one who stands firm to the end will be saved. And this gospel of the kingdom will be preached in the whole world as a testimony to all nations, and then the end will come. (Matthew 24:12–14 NIV)

CHAPTER 5

The Seed of Abraham

> Now the promises (covenants, agreements) were decreed and made to Abraham and his Seed (his Offspring, his Heir). He [God] does not say, And to seeds (descendants, heirs), as if referring to many persons, but, And to your Seed (your Descendant, your Heir), obviously referring to one individual, Who is [none other than] Christ (the Messiah). (Galatians 3:16 AMPC)

After the death of Terah's son Haran, he took Abram and his son's wife Sarai and Haran's son Lot to the land of Haran. They left their homeland of Ur of the Chaldeans in order to enter the land of Canaan, but Terah settled in the land of Haran. *Ironically, Terah died where he settled (see Genesis 11:31–32).* The LORD God saw the faith in Abram and instructed him to leave his father's house and journey to the land that would be shown to him. Abram was obedient to the divine declaration. Once Abram left the land of Haran and entered Canaan, then the LORD God appeared to him.

When the time came for Abram and Lot to separate, Lot was given the freedom to choose where he would settle, yet Abram never left Canaan. After separating from Lot, the LORD God vowed the land of Canaan to Abram and his defendants after him. The LORD would respond to Abram according to his level of obedience by actually appearing, or in a vision, or in a dream of the night. In turn, Abram would purposely build an altar as a memorial to the LORD and a reminder of His word.

After Abram's war with the enemy kings to recover all, including Lot and his family, he gave a tithe to the LORD from the hands of Melchizedek, king of Salem. Not only was Melchizedek a king, but he was a priest of God Most High. Melchizedek presented Abram with a *covenant meal* (bread and wine) and then blessed him with the name of God Most High.

Later, the LORD came to Abram in a vision and said, "Do not fear, Abram, I am a shield to you; your reward shall be great" (Genesis 15:1 NASB). In the vision, the LORD promised him a son and gave instructions on how to present an offering in order to come into *covenant* with the LORD. Once the offering was made, Abram had a night vision and was given the revelation of the enslavement of his descendants, the judgment of the nation who would enslave them, and the fulfillment of the promise that the fourth generation would return to Canaan.

Even after Abram and Sarai sinned by trying to bring the LORD's word to pass in their own strength, the delay was not a denial from the Almighty. The LORD was merciful and appeared again to Abram when he was ninety-nine and said, "I am God Almighty; walk before Me, and be blameless. And I will establish My covenant between Me and you, and I will multiply you exceedingly" (Genesis 17:1–2 NASB). In this redemptive exchange, the Almighty changed Abram's name to *Abraham (father of a multitude of nations)*, and Sarai's name was changed to *Sarah (mother of nations)*. At this time, the Almighty inaugurated *circumcision* as *a sign of the covenant.* That same day, Abraham and the men under his authority who were eight days old and older were circumcised.

After Abraham was completely healed from his circumcision, the LORD appeared with two angels by the oaks of Mamre. Abraham lifted up his eyes as he sat at his tent door and saw three men standing opposite of him. Abraham ran to meet them and bowed down before the LORD, requesting that the LORD would not pass him by, to rest under the tree, and be refreshed with a meal. Quickly, Abraham prepared the best of all he had, presented it to them, and *stood by them under the tree as they ate*. Normally, Sarah would have waited on them as their custom would dictate, but this was an offering to the LORD. Once their meal was completed, the LORD declared, "I will surely return to you at this time next year, and Sarah your wife will have a son" (Genesis 18:10a NASB).

Isaac was born according to the word of the LORD. Sometime later, Ishmael and his mother Hagar were removed from the only home that they knew by the word of Sarah and confirmed by the Almighty. Once Isaac grew to be a young man, the Almighty challenged the obedience of Abraham by requesting that Isaac be offered up to him.

Now prior to the LORD's promise of a son, Abraham saw the life of the only begotten son of God.

Jesus stated, "Your father Abraham rejoiced to see My day, and he saw it and was glad" (John 8:56 NASB). Abraham saw in the vision the birth, death, and resurrection of Jesus. He was fully persuaded that the Almighty could raise the dead as he saw Jesus being raised. The question was not in the Almighty's ability but in Abraham's total obedience to not withhold the dearest thing of his heart from the LORD. We are all aware that Abraham, our "father of faith," passed the test. Jesus, who is the "Seed of Promise," declares, "He who loves father or mother more than me is not worthy of Me; and he who loves son or daughter more than Me is not worthy of Me. And he who does not take up his cross and follow after Me is not worthy of Me" (Matthew 10:37–38 NASB).

The significant point that the Holy Spirit is making is that he *expects swift obedience from all who belong to him in Christ Jesus*. No one is prepared for what is coming upon the earth, not even "the remnant church." We will be given divine strategies, resources, and protection as we align with his Word. Those who settle are like those who walk contrary to his will, for rebellion is the spirit of witchcraft…being out of alignment could lead to death.

Every promise that the LORD God made to Abram, he faithfully fulfilled. Abraham, our "father of faith," *immediately obeyed* the divine instructions and left his father's land, believed the promises of God, separated from Lot, obtained a divine promise for a son, and entered into a covenant with the Most High God. In this new season, many of us will be commanded to do things that may seem foolish, but revelation will be imparted as we quickly move in the will of God.

The promises of God are yes and amen, and they are also generational. The land of Canaan was promised to Abraham and to his descendants after him. Abram's father, Terah, had the same opportunity, *but he settled for a land that wasn't promised to him*. Through the obedience of Abram, he took hold of the mantle that his father failed to carry in order to produce a generational blessing for those who would come after him.

We, "the remnant church," are partnering with the Almighty to build, tear down, uproot, plant, and pick up mantles that will command a blessing for the generations that will come after us. We have an awesome opportunity to further the kingdom of God in the earthly realm. The commanded blessing from *El Shaddai—"The All-Sufficient One:"*

> And I will bless those who bless you, and the one who curses you I will curse. And in you all the families of the earth shall be blessed. (Genesis 12:3 NASB)

In this new season, the body of Christ will be separated from the "familiar things" in order to receive the "new things" that the Almighty has for us. "The remnant church" remains in the promises of God and walks in total obedience. We can expect him to manifest his multifaceted love according to our individual and corporate levels of obedience. Our memorials will not be of stone but will be tender hearts toward him, and he will give us his blueprints for the generations to come.

> Unless the LORD builds the house, they labor in vain who build it; unless the LORD guards the city, the watchman keeps awake in vain. (Psalm 127:1 NASB)

CHAPTER 6

Melchizedek

And Melchizedek the king of Salem brought out bread and wine; now he was a priest of God Most High. And he blessed him and said, "Blessed be Abram of God Most High, Possessor of heaven and earth; And blessed be God Most High, who has handed over your enemies to you." And he gave him a tenth of everything. (Genesis 14:18–20 NASB)

After the fall of man, mankind started to seek the LORD God again. Because of sin, mankind no longer knew the ways of God. Through the great loving-kindness of the LORD God, he sent angels to teach mankind of his ways. The scriptures refer to these angels as the "Sons of God." These divine beings had flesh on them so that they could commune with mankind. Unfortunately, many of them transgressed their covenant with The Almighty by procreating with the daughters of man. In doing so, it created a corrupt hybrid race referred to as the *Nephilim*.

Not all the "Sons of God" fell into this abominable act with mankind. There were a few that held faithfully to the LORD God Almighty. Likewise, there were eight righteous persons who had not been corrupted by crossbreeding. Noah was found righteous in the sight of God. He and his family were chosen to preserve all the living creatures that were appointed to accompany Noah and his family in the ark. After the flood, Noah's sons, Shem, Ham, and Japheth, were used to repopulate the earth with mankind.

In the genealogies, only the firstborn male's name is recorded. Noah was blessed with triplets: Shem, Ham, and Japheth. Many scholars believe that Melchizedek was Shem, the son of Noah. This theory contradicts the word of God. The holy scriptures do confirm that Shem was alive in the time of Abram who was later known as Abraham. Abraham was a descendant of Shem, according to 1 Chronicles 1:17–27. Shem died according to this:

> This is the account of Shem's family line. Two years after the flood, when Shem was 100 years old, he became the father of Arphaxad. And after he became the father of Arphaxad, Shem lived 500 years and had other sons and daughters. (Genesis 11:10–11 NIV)

In the New Testament, the Apostle Paul teaches on Melchizedek in *Hebrews 7:3* and *7:16*. Paul points out the criteria that had to be made: *Hebrews 7:3* says without father or mother, without genealogy, having neither beginning of days nor end of life but made like the Son of God, he abides a priest perpetually. *Hebrews 7:16* refers to an indestructible life. This New Testament reference agrees with the word of the Almighty concerning his only begotten son, Jesus Christ.

> This Melchizedek was king of Salem and priest of God Most High. He met Abraham returning from the defeat of the kings and blessed him, and Abraham gave him a tenth of everything. First, the name Melchizedek means "king of righteousness;" then also, "king of Salem" means "king of peace." (Hebrews 7:1–2 NIV)

In Genesis 6:2, the scriptures refer to the "Sons of God," who were angels covered with flesh and who were sent from the LORD

God to teach mankind his ways. As stated earlier, not all the "Sons of God" transgressed against the LORD God. Now referring to the scripture above (Hebrews 7:1–2), the authority of a king is to carry out the law of God, but the authority of the priest is to teach the law of God.

The Old Testament conceals the mystery of Christ, yet the New Testament reveals Christ. Keeping this in mind, as we park in Hebrews 7:3, the latter half of this verse states, "But made like the Son of God, he abides a priest perpetually." Are we saying then that Melchizedek was Jesus? Absolutely not.

The likeness of something is just an imagery of the authentic. Based on the scriptural accounts, both have flesh and are called the Son of God. Being the Son of God denotes an indestructible life.

Now *Jesus* is the Word made flesh and dwelt among us, and *he is the only begotten Son of the Father* according to John chapter one. Our statement is that before Melchizedek, it was Jesus. We are stating that Melchizedek was the imagery of who possessed similar roles that would authentically be revealed in Jesus. To reemphasize, Melchizedek is not Jesus.

Then who is Melchizedek? One of the "Sons of God" who did not transgress the command of the LORD God. In the book of Exodus 25:40, God commanded Moses by saying, "See that you make them after the pattern for them, which was shown to you on the mountain."

This divine statement from the Almighty did not just concern the tabernacle, the furnishings, or the priestly garments but also the structure of authority for each role, be it for the priests or the laymen. This was also emphasized in Hebrews 8:5 NASB, "Who serves as a copy and shadow of the heavenly things, just as Moses was warned by God when he was about to erect the tabernacle for 'see,' He says 'that you make all things by the pattern which was shown to you on the mountain.'"

Only the high priest has the authority to minister before the Almighty. The priests were the only ones who could offer incense to God Most High. Those who were of priestly lineage but offered up strange fire were instantly killed (Leviticus 10:1–3). Now according to the heavenly pattern, when 250 laymen attempted to offer incense, it cost them their very lives (see Numbers 16).

> As a reminder to the sons of Israel so that <u>no layman</u>, anyone who was not of the descendants of Aaron, would approach to burn incense before the LORD; then he would not become like Korah and his group—just as the LORD had spoken to him through Moses. (Numbers 16:40 NASB)

Revelations 8:3–5 mentions an angel who had the authority to offer incense before the Almighty. Melchizedek's name wasn't mentioned, but his role as a priest to God Most High was emphasized.

> <u>Another angel</u> came and stood at the altar, holding a golden censer; and much incense was given to him, so that he might add it to the prayers of all the saints on the golden altar which was before the throne. And the smoke of the incense ascended from the angel's hand with the prayers of the saints before God. Then the angel took the censer and filled it with the fire of the altar and hurled it to the earth; and there were peals of thunder and sounds, and flashes of lightning and an earthquake. (Revelation 8:3–5 NASB)

In conclusion, Melchizedek is a Son of God who ministers to God Most High as a priest in the heavenly sanctuary. Based on Revelations 8:3–5, he seems to be the *only angel* who has been granted authority from God Most High to offer incense in his holy presence. The heavenly pattern thus agrees with the earthly pattern. Melchizedek is a priest to God Most High forever.

CHAPTER 7

The Seed of the Word

> But I tell you, on the day of judgment men will have to give account for every idle (inoperative, nonworking) word they speak. For by your words you will be justified and acquitted, and by your words you will be condemned and sentenced. (Matthew 12:36–37 AMPC)

In the beginning, the Almighty declared, "Let there be," and it came into existence by the Word. We (mankind) were created in the image and likeness of God. As the Almighty created the invisible and visible realms with the Word, he has given us the authority to cultivate our world with our words. *Our words are so powerful!* When a word of encouragement is given, our hearts are filled with joy, but if a word of discouragement is given, then our hearts are saddened. This is why the Word of God instructs us to guard our hearts. The very words we speak go into the souls of the listener(s). By our words, we can cultivate healing or destruction in the lives of those around us, as well as ourselves.

The spoken Word of God or our words can either restore our souls or cause trauma. Many people can go through a bout of illness and can be healed from it. Unfortunately, because of the trauma to our souls, we sometimes can't embrace the full healing. After being healed from several health issues, I heard Jesus say, *"You are so used to being broken that when I healed you, you rejected it!"* To hear the anguish and longing for wholeness for me in Jesus's voice broke me. I cried out, *"What must I do? Teach me how to receive full healing."* The Spirit of God then led me on my first seven-day fast. I asked to be strengthened in this new endeavor, and the Holy Spirit said, *"Whatever is strengthened by the Word is sustained by the Word."*

Why is fasting important? It is a powerful tool to help us to realign with the source…the Almighty. If your car is out of alignment, it can make your journey rough.

If the dis-alignment is not fixed in a timely manner, it can hinder staying safely on your journey while causing other major issues for the car. The scriptures never said if you fast, but when you fast. Fasting denies the flesh while the Spirit is being edified by the Word of God. "Man shall not live on bread alone, but on every word that comes out of the mouth of God" (Matthew 4:4 NASB). During the fast, many areas of great trauma to our souls are revealed. The Holy Spirit needed these areas to be exposed, released, and then filled with the sweet fruit of his light.

> But the fruit of the Spirit is (love, joy, peace, patience, kindness, goodness, faithfulness, gentleness, and self-control. (Galatians 5:22–23)

Soul trauma causes darkness to flood our inner man. Fasting helps to expose those areas so that the light of the Holy Spirit can rid us of all darkness. We are called to be children of light, for the Almighty is the Father of lights, and we are his offspring. True healing comes when the source of the dis-alignment is revealed and uprooted. Once the exposed area of darkness is uprooted, the enemy can no longer use it as leverage to keep us bound. Have we not read, for whom the Son has set free is free indeed? (For more revelation on this subject, see the *second chapter* of my book, "The Anointing: How to Walk in the Limitless Power of God.")

Fasting is one of the divine tools to aid us in living a submitted, committed, and consecrated life. *"Submit yourselves therefore to God. Resist the devil, and he will flee from you" (James 4:7*

KJV). Fasting increases our ability to clearly identify and hear the voice of the Living God. We, as the body of Christ, are ill-prepared for the exceptionally gross darkness that is coming upon the earth. When we regularly humble ourselves under the mighty hand of God through this divine key of fasting, then the LORD of Host will give us strategies. We cannot afford to operate with slowness of heart or dullness of hearing. Things are happening at an accelerated pace, and the LORD of Host expects swift and complete obedience to his Word.

The Word of God is another divine tool. It is so sad to discover how many people do not know the Word of God, yet they deem themselves as followers of Christ Jesus. The Word of God is Spirit, and it is life. How can something be spiritually appraised apart from the Word? *Answer: It can't.* Unfortunately, some have entertained doctrines of demons as if it were the Word of the Living God. The Almighty, Jesus, nor the Holy Spirit will ever speak contrary to the written Word of God. Even the Apostle Paul warned the church that another doctrine given by men or angels that contradicted the Word of the Living God is to be viewed as accursed (Galatians 1:8).

The fivefold ministry (apostle, prophet, evangelist, pastor, teacher) was initiated by the will of God to edify and instruct the body of Christ (Ephesians 4:11). Our relationship with our LORD and Savior is our own individual responsibility. As stated before, we can't know the voice of God if we don't know his Word. When we assemble ourselves with other believers as his Word teaches, we should receive confirmations of the Word that we have meditated on in private. In this faith-filled moment of fellowship, iron is sharpening iron, a greater level of faith is imparted, and it gives birth to revelation.

The Almighty is always speaking to us, but we are not always attuned to his voice. The various distractions that we face daily can cause us to slow our hearts and even have dullness of hearing. Like our LORD Jesus, who purposely pursued the Father, we are to imitate what he did. Jesus fasted often to keep his soul submitted to his spirit versus his flesh. The Almighty is gentle and loving yet sovereign and holy. He (the Almighty) will not compete with a noisy soul, for he has given us authority to guard our own hearts or souls. He commands us, *"Be still and know that he is God!"*

During a very challenging time in my life, it produced such a burden to break free from debt. *Debt is a curse* (see Deuteronomy 28:44, Proverbs 22:7, and Romans 13:8)! Many are faithful tithers but still find themselves drowning in debt. Debt is not always caused by poor management of funds. Sometimes, this is a generational stronghold that needs to be broken. In an earnest effort to resolve this issue, the Holy One led me to go on a fast. On the third day of the fast, the LORD allowed teaching to hit my Internet feed on this very subject. A well-known faith-based ministry was teaching "From Owing to Owning."

Here's my personal testimony with the Word that broke the spirit of debt off my life.

Word applied debt-free testimony.

I took the Word that was taught and lifted the scriptures up to Jesus and said, "All right, LORD, show me where I'm missing it."

Jesus replied, *"Your mouth."*

What? Every careless word that we speak that is contrary to the Word of God, the devil uses against us. We have courts on earth because we have courts in heaven. The heavenly Father intends to bless his children because it brings him great pleasure. The law of the Almighty will not allow him to go against our will. Like the Word of God is his will, so our words are our will.

Here's an example of a daily scripture, "The LORD's prayer:"

> Our Father who art in heaven, Hallowed be Thy name, Thy kingdom come, Thy will be done, on earth as it is in heaven. Give us this day our daily bread, and forgive us our debts, as we also have forgiven our debtors, and do not lead us into temptation, but deliver us from evil. For Thine is the kingdom, and the power, and the glory, forever, Amen. (Matthew 6:9–14 NASB)

This is a daily prayer of mine. Jesus showed me that the Father has already forgiven me of my debts; however, when we claim debt by our own words, we have nullified our prayer to the Father.

Our word is a seed of our will, and by it, we can sow debt into our lives. The evil one will take our words to the courts of heaven and state his case against us. The Almighty is bound by our words until we repent and renounce them. The short of it is that Jesus taught me how to clean up my spoken words before *declaring* what he said in his Word. How do we clean our words? *By repentance.*

Here's a simple prayer that the Holy One gave me to clean my words.

> Almighty Father,
>
> I repent, rebuke, and renounce every careless word that I have spoken that is not in alignment with your will, which is your Word. I declare that every verbal contract that I established with the evil one is null and void. I submit and realign my words to your Word, which is your perfect will in the mighty name of Jesus. Amen.

This process taught me to focus on the words of my mouth, yield to the Holy Spirit, and allow him to convict me throughout my day of any wrong words that were spoken. This process took a six-month period, and now this is done twice a day (morning and evening) before my special times with my LORD. Let me reemphasize this important point: whatever we have repented of and given to God, we cannot take back!

Example: If someone asks you if you owe anything, simply say, "The Almighty is graciously covering that expense." It doesn't matter what the debt is: a mortgage on a home, a car note, a lease on a building, etc. What if you are short on cash? Simply state, "I don't have that at this moment." This is just a simple way of expressing God's ownership of the debt.

Now this does not exempt you from paying the bill. The Father of Lights will provide the seed or financial resources you need. During this six-month time frame, these principles were applied to my finances, and the manifestation of what was declared was obtained within three days. The more my faith aligned with the LORD's word, the more manifestation started to occur on the same day. My debt was over $15,000+, and the plan was to pay it off within a five- to six-year time frame.

As I went on the fourth month of this six-month time frame, my debt concerns and finances were relinquished to the authority of the Father. Seeking the Father for wisdom in this area of debt and giving him total authority over all my finances was a game changer for me. He knows the end from the beginning and can forewarn us of any pitfalls that are coming on the horizon.

Quickly, here are two true stories.

Story #1: There was a light bill that came in the mail, but it wasn't due for a couple of weeks. The Father had given me the resources to pay the bill, but I inquired for his direction. There was a strong sense of "wait." (Just a sidenote: When we ask the Almighty Father for direction, we must yield to what he speaks.) Three days went by, and on my way home, my driver-side front tire experienced a flat. There was a tire store a block away, and the amount of the tire was similar to the amount of the light bill.

The next day was my payday, and then the Father gave me peace about paying the light bill. See, our Father knows the end from the beginning!

Story #2: Many times, companies will send in a lower consolidated bill for different reasons, and this happens to me on one particular bill. Inquiring for direction from the Almighty is now a way of life, and in my stillness, a louder "wait" from the Holy One was received. When the weekend arrived, there was another letter from the same company that was offering more than half of the original consolidated amount. Then there was a strong sense of "now pay it." Because of obedience to the voice of my God, it produced a greater surplus that was applied to other bills.

The Father rocked my world! In ninety days, my heavenly Father canceled *all* debt! What would have taken me five to six years to do only took my Almighty Papa ninety days. Praise God! *I owe no man but to love him.* The Word of God does work! We must clean up our words and align them with the Word and expect our God to do what only he can.

Many reading this testimony may think well, that's good, but that won't happen for me. Throughout the gospels, Jesus (who is the Word of God) declared, *"Be it done according to your faith!"* If you believe in debt, you will continue to receive it. In 2 Corinthian 9:8, it states, "God is able to make all grace abound to you, so that always having all sufficiency in *everything*, you may have an abundance for every good deed/work." Please understand that it has nothing to do with how much resources or money that you have. We, the "church," do not rely on the world's system but the kingdom's economy. What's that, you may ask? It's the Word of God declared in faith.

God is the one who gives the seed. The Seed is the Word that covers every area of one's life, be it spiritual, physical, or financial. When our words are aligned with the Word of God in faith, then manifestation takes place. *Your blessing is in your mouth!* We must learn to walk in our kingly authority and *declare a thing, and God will establish it according to his will (Job 22:28).*

> "And it will come about in that day that I will respond," declares the LORD. "I will respond to the heavens, and they will respond to the earth, and the earth will respond to the grain, to the new wine, and to the oil, and they will respond to Jezreel." (Hosea 2:21–22 NASB)

CHAPTER 8

The Signs of the Times

> He replied, "When evening comes, you say, 'It
> will be fair weather, for the sky is red,' and in the
> morning, 'Today it will be stormy, for the sky is
> red and overcast.' You know how to interpret the
> appearance of the sky, but you cannot interpret
> the signs of the times." (Matthew 16:2–3 NIV)

We are transitioning from the dispensation of grace into the last days when we enter into the year 2020/5780 on the Jewish calendar. Not only was it a pivotal new decade, but it was also a powerful prophetic era. We ushered in the "decade of the mouth." In the first quarter of this new decade, the "power of fear" gripped the entire world. Because of this demonic *power,* we were made to cover our mouths with masks.

> Death and life are in the power of the tongue:
> and they that love it shall eat the fruit thereof.
> (Psalm 18:21 KJV)

Ironically, the very era in which we were encouraged to declare the Word of God started with trying to silence us. Many seemingly watched helplessly as the darkness quickly turned into gross darkness. As the darkness covered the earth simultaneously, the remnant church arose, declaring the Word of God in the name of Jesus. The Word of God, in Jesus's name, is the only way that this demonic *power* was pushed back. In Ephesians 1:21, we are reminded that the name of *Jesus* is above all *rule* and *authority* and *power* and *dominion* and *every name that is named*. As mentioned earlier, the "power of fear" crippled the entire world until the Word of God in the name of Jesus was declared. Greater is he who is within us than he who is within the world.

The Almighty, through his servants and the prophets for decades, has given warning after warning, but the Church refused to wake up. He declares, "Awake, O sleeper, and arise from the dead, and Christ will shine on you" (Ephesians 5:14).

Jesus has already given us victory, but we must be sober and alert on this evil day. Many may think that this is the worst that it can get. *Wrong!* This is just the beginning of what is to come. Remember that serpent of old who is the devil who prials around like a lion seeking whom he may devour. The evil one knows that his time is short, so trust and believe he will not go down without a fight. *The evil one is already defeated!* What is coming next, we are not prepared for, nor can we comprehend. This is a time to seek the Almighty for strategy.

> Proclaim this among the nations: Prepare for holy war; stir up the warriors! Have all the soldiers come forward, have them come up! (Joel 3:9 NASB)

The Almighty desires to release divine downloads, but we must be in the correct posture to receive. We must make up our minds to walk in a consecrated lifestyle that is humbly and wholly committed and submitted to the Almighty. He commands us to be holy as he is holy. Once we humbly come before the LORD God with clean hands and a pure heart, he will then endow us with revelatory wisdom like the sons of Issachar. The sons of Issachar were men who understood the times and knew what Israel should do.

Many false prophets have risen in these days and have caused many to doubt the word of the prophet. Saints, we must try the spirit by the Spirit to see if it is of God. We must know the Word of God for ourselves. The LORD God will *never speak contrary* to his written Word. His written Word will always align with the message that he releases through his servants, the prophets. The Almighty is calling us to be totally submitted to the leading and guidance of the Holy Spirit. The Spirit of Truth will impart revelation from the heart of the Father, empower, and bring unity into the body of Christ Jesus (the church).

The Holy Spirit directed me to study Jesus's transfiguration on the mountain in Luke 9:28–36 as an example of what's coming. In this passage of scripture, *Jesus took Peter, James, and John up onto a mountain to pray.* Jesus was transformed before them and was accompanied by Moses and Elijah.

Moses was used by the LORD God to bring deliverance from bondage for Israel, and he also taught the written commandments, decrees, and laws of God. The Holy Spirit emphasized the deliverance of the Israelites who were under Egyptian bondage. The focus was to be on Exodus chapters 11–14. This is what the Spirit of God revealed:

Like in the days of Moses when the outstretched hand of God rendered judgment, so it will be. The LORD God released ten plagues on Egypt (*water turned to blood, frogs, gnats, flies, death to the livestock in the field, festering boils, hailstorms, locusts, darkness that can be felt, every firstborn son of Egypt and cattle will die: "death angel"*).

The Israelites went through the first three plagues (*water turned to blood, frogs, gnats*) before the LORD God made a distinction between them and the Egyptians. Although *the Israelites also went through the first three plagues, the LORD gave them special instructions* so that they did not suffer as the Egyptians did.

When it came to the last plague, the Israelites were given specific instructions on how to prepare the sacrificial lamb, which was to be a year-old male without defect. They were given instructions on how to prepare the meat of the slaughtered lamb without blemish and how to apply the blood on the doors of the homes.

All who took refuge within the dwellings of the Israelites were safe from the "angel of death." All who ate the lamb received miraculous healing, for the Word states, "That there were no feeble among them" (Psalm 105:37). After the "angel of death" killed all the firstborn of the Egyptians and their cattle, then the LORD God gave the Israelites the order to plunder all the wealth of the Egyptians.

The glory of the LORD God was upon his people, and there was no sick or feeble among them. Israel was led out of Egypt by the strong hand of God. They were soon pursued by the Egyptian army. The waters of the Red Sea were parted by the blast of the Almighty's nostril, and Israel walked across on dry land. However, when the enemy attempted it, they were destroyed. The declaration was *The enemy you see today you will not see tomorrow.*

So what does that have to do with what's coming, you may ask? In a similar manner, the Israelites in Goshen were affected by the first three plagues, but through obeying the instructions of the LORD, they were not affected as the Egyptians. What has been released will affect the remnant church, but as we yield to the directions of the Almighty, this will bring preservation.

There is a plague similar to the "angel of death" that has been released on the earth. This is not going to be like the plague in 2020. This plague is deadly and will kill quickly. The blood of Jesus, who is our sacrificial lamb, will cover the remnant church and the nations who are under our prayerful covering.

The wealth transfer will happen overnight while a revival of healing will hit the earth. *No man will lead this healing revival.* The LORD God will bring this about in his own divine way. The greatest darkness ever known to man will appear. We will then be ushered into a baptism of the greater glory of God. This baptism of the glory will transform us into the sons and daughters of God for whom the earth has been travailing. This particular enemy that pursues "the remnant church" will be no more.

The second part of the revelation of Jesus's transformation on the mountain concerns Elijah. *Elijah* was a prophet of God who declared judgment on the king and religious leaders in his day for defying the laws and standards set by the Living God. The Spirit of

God was emphasized in 1 Kings chapter 18. During this time, the LORD God gave Elijah authority through prayer to bring about a drought that produced famine in the land.

The famine lasted for three and a half years. Elijah, led by the Spirit, came out of hiding and challenged King Ahab, the religious leaders, and the people under him to a demonstration. All of Israel was gathered at Mount Carmel together with 450 prophets of Baal and 400 prophets of the Asherah, all those who ate at Jezebel's table. The god who answered by fire would be deemed the true and living God. This demonstration would be a witness to the people of Israel so that the people would turn back to the LORD God.

There were two altars built and two offerings presented. Neither party could put fire to their offering but had to call on the name of their god. The God who answers by fire is the true and living God. The prophets of Baal cried out with loud voices, leaped around, and cut themselves until blood gushed forth. They continued this spectacle from morning to noon and then finally to the evening.

Elijah then repaired the altar of the LORD, which had been torn down. He then took twelve stones according to the number of tribes of Israel, built a trench around the altar, and ordered those four pitchers of water to be poured on the offering three times. He then called on the name of the LORD, and the fire of God consumed the burnt offering, the wood, the stones, and the dust. He licked up the water that was in the trench. Elijah then ordered that the wicked prophets be slaughtered at the Kishon Brook.

There was a prophetic utterance given to Elijah after the slaughter of the false prophets. He declared to King Ahab, "There is a sound of the roar of a heavy shower." Elijah went back up to the top of Mount Carmel, postured himself with his face between his knees, and then sent his servant to look toward the sea. After seven attempts, his servant finally declared, "A cloud as small as a man's hand is coming up from the sea."

Like in the days of Elijah, the entire world is in a spiritual famine. The LORD God will judge the church in a similar manner as the prophets of Baal and Asherah, these leaders who have turned the hearts of the people from following the LORD God. They have eaten at Jezebel's table, they have welcomed this demonic spirit into the sanctuary, and they have turned the houses of God into the *Assemblies of Satan.*

The LORD God has given time for these leaders to repent, but they refused.

Please understand that the prophets of Baal and Asherah represent the false leadership in the church. Those who refuse to repent will be destroyed in a similar manner of judgment.

The "greater glory" will be born out of a dark time, which was represented by the heavy showers. The enemy will speak out a threat like the spirit of Jezebel, but we can't retreat in fear like Elijah. The Almighty is commanding us to be very strong and courageous. We will stand and behold the salvation of the LORD.

The final reflection on the mountain of transfiguration was when Jesus was seen in his glorified state by Peter, James, and John. A time is coming when the church will see Jesus as he truly is and will be in awe of his splendor and majesty. From that divine encounter, the fear of the LORD will engulf "the remnant church" as the cloud of glory enveloped the disciples. The divine declaration from the Almighty, "This is my Son, whom I have chosen; listen to him" (Luke 9:35). This divine revelation from the Almighty is our strategy to push back the darkness.

"The Word became flesh and dwelt among us; and we saw His glory, glory as of the only Son from the Father, full of grace and truth" (John 1:14). Jesus is the Word of God. We must be so focused on Jesus that we set our face like flint in his direction. We can't afford any distractions. This is a spiritual war that we are in. We can't foolishly look to the government of man for the answers, but we must seek the government of the Almighty God.

> Surely the arm of the LORD is not too short to save, nor his ear too dull to hear. But your iniquities have separated you from your God; your sins have hidden his face from you, so that he will not hear. For your hands are stained with blood, your

fingers with guilt. Your lips have spoken falsely,
and your tongue mutters wicked things. (Isaiah
59:1–3 NIV)

Warning Word of the LORD
July 17, 2022

The LORD God showed me a picture of an elected official and a Middle Eastern prince bumping fists. The LORD God declared, "Payment has now been made," to start the Internet virus in order to hold captive this nation and the world. There is another virus being released that will kill fast and is very deadly. It will be two simultaneous viruses that will hit not just the United States but the world.

But God! But God! He is also going to redeem his people and is in the process of judging his church. Those who have *not* walked according to the will of God and have eaten at Jezebel's table. The LORD has said, "They shall be removed because they are not of Me! They are not of Me!" So as the prophet Elijah stood firm and declared, thus says the LORD, there are prophets who, after the order of Elijah, warned the church body to repent, especially the leaders.

Now it is time for judgment! The LORD God is judging his people, and he is starting with leadership. In 2019, the spirit of the LORD said, "Those who have been in leadership for years and who are hindering the move of the living God will be removed! Some will retire, some will step down, and some will be removed by death." This word was given in September of 2019. The fullness of understanding did not manifest until 2020.

The Word of the LORD said, "It will not be so as it was in 2020." God is going to remove multiple because he has given them time to repent and change their ways. They have refused to repent! They have been stiff-necked, so the LORD God himself will remove them personally. Those who have womanized their flock, adultery, witchcraft, fornication, entertained Jezebel, welcomed Jezebel into the sanctuary, and pushed out the spirit of the Living God.

God is going to have his way! He's going to close many, many churches that call themselves a church, but they were not churches but *Assemblies of Satan*. The Spirit of the Living God is going to refine the church in order to purify her because she is stained thoroughly with the sins of the world. He said, "Come out from among her my people, come out from among her my people, come out from among her my people, says the Living God!"

Like in the days of Elijah, as well as in the days of Moses, this move is not going to be like any other move. There will be two simultaneous deaths that will occur. God is going to judge his people! God is going to judge his people like he did in the days of Elijah. Those prophets who ate at Jezebel's table and turned, turned, turned the people against the LORD God Almighty. They turned the people toward Baal, Molech, and Asherah. They died altogether on the same day so the wrath of God would return and be executed in a similar manner.

Like the days of Moses, when the death angel came through and killed all the firstborns of the Egyptians, including their cattle, so it will be. For the plagues that have started, the Almighty God will check because the blood of Jesus will have stayed over those that are of the remnant of his people. Under that remnant covering, households will be saved of different nationalities; households will be saved like it was in Goshen. So shall it be in the United States; so shall it be throughout the world. The spirit of the LORD God has spoken. Amen.

> Arise, shine; for your light has come, and the glory of the LORD has risen upon you. For behold, darkness will cover the earth and deep darkness the peoples; but the LORD will rise upon you and His glory will appear upon you. Nations will come to your light, and kings to the brightness of your rising. Raise your eyes all around and see; they all gather together, they come to you. Your sons will come from afar, and your daughters will be carried on the hip. Then you will see and be radiant, and your heart will thrill and rejoice; because the abundance of the sea will be turned to you, the wealth of the nations will come to you. (Isaiah 60:1–5 NASB)

CHAPTER 9

The Shaking

> Therefore, I will make the heavens tremble, and
> the earth will be shaken from its place at the fury
> of the LORD of armies in the day of His burning
> anger. (Isaiah 13:13 NASB)

There are ancient principalities that have been released in the earth's realm. These demonic forces are always identified through child sacrifice that then gives birth to every form of sexual immorality and perversion, like in the days when Israel was given their land by inheritance the following seven nations: *Hittites, Girgashites, Amorites, Canaanites, Perizzites, Hivites, and Jebusites.* They were marked for destruction due to this kind of perversion (see Deuteronomy 7:1–2).

> Do not pollute the land where you are. Bloodshed
> pollutes the land, and atonement cannot be made
> for the land on which blood has been shed, except
> by the blood of the one who shed it. (Numbers
> 35:33 NIV)

One of the most powerful empires in the world was the Roman Empire, and they no longer exist because they, too, like the previous seven nations, practiced the same detestable lifestyles. This is *not* a political message but a warning given by the Almighty to be considered as a divine principle. Yes, Jesus died for the world, for without the shedding of blood, there is no remission of sin. Now "the church" has allowed herself to be stained by these immoral acts and has conformed to the sins of the world, and because of these practices, it has lost her identity.

How did this happen? The spirit of the Living God brings unity. The religion of man grieved and quenched the Holy Spirit by not allowing him to flow freely in the church or in the home. The evil one was given the opportunity to bring about discord, which led to division. This division caused a dismantling of the family unit by removing the men from the homes. The slow moral decay caused a breach to happen in the church, which gave way to allowing moral decay to take root. The moral decay led to the religious legalism of man, which gave birth to rebellion, and the rebellion then gave birth to every form of sexual immorality, which led to perversion in the church. Division is always a tactic of the evil one, but unity is the will of the Father that brings a blessing.

> Behold, how good and how pleasant it is for brethren to dwell together in unity!
>
> It is like the precious oil upon the head, running down on the beard, the beard of Aaron, running down on the edge of his garments. It is like the dew of Hermon, descending upon the mountains of Zion; for there the LORD commanded the blessing—life forevermore. (Psalm 133:1–3 KJV)

The United States is the only other nation besides Israel that was founded on the powerful name of God. It is a "spiritual Israel." What does this have to do with the church? *Everything!* Salvation is from the Jews (John 4:22). The church has forsaken her first love, *Jesus*. The church has lost the awe and reverential fear of the LORD. Our identity as the church is connected to this revelation, which is given by the Holy Spirit to help us maintain the awe and reverential fear of the LORD.

A shake-up for a wake-up!

This process can be compared to how olives are harvested. The olive tree is violently shaken. The ripe olives that fall to the ground are gathered and then placed into the press to be crushed. Like Jesus in the garden of Gethsemane (which means olive press) experienced crushing, which reveals the anointing he carried prior to his crucifixion. So you see that this process awakens us to the anointing that we already carry. The same anointing that raised Christ from the dead is in every true blood-washed believer of Christ Jesus.

The LORD God is using these shakings as a tool or method for separation. Yes, the LORD loves unity but will use this shaking to identify who truly belongs to him or not. This separation process can be likened to the removal of impurities in metal (like silver) before the purification process can begin. According to *Malachi 3:3, he sits as a smelter and purifier of silver and a refiner of gold.*

Through the various shakings of things that are created, the LORD God will reintroduce to us his mighty power. As we faithfully posture ourselves in a humbled position at his feet of complete surrender, he will then open the eyes of our hearts to see him as he is. The LORD delivered a warning rebuke; *he will not accept a conditional surrender to him.* He desires for us to empty ourselves of all cares and desires so that he may fill us in the purity of his love in these same areas.

The Almighty is breaking down every wall of division. He is adamant about breaking down the wall of males versus females. Jesus redeemed his daughters when his side was pierced on the cross. In that moment, Jesus restored the woman's rightful authority to rule and reign in this earthly realm in unity with man. Together, we are to push back the darkness and further the kingdom of God on earth.

Anytime the Almighty desires something to be birthed on earth, he always uses the womb of a woman. Examples of this were when God desired a nation of his own possession, Isaac was birthed through the barren womb of Sarah. God desired for a prophet to walk before him to govern Israel, and he brought Samuel forth from the barren womb of Hannah. At the end of Israel's enslavement in Egypt, God needed a deliverer for his people, so Moses was born from Jochebed. Lastly, the world needed a savior, so he sent himself (Jesus) and came through the womb of the Virgin Mary.

There is a sound that only a woman can make as she travails, which moves the heart of God. A woman's travail tells heaven that God's promise is being birthed. Hannah groaned in prayer before God in the temple, and heaven released Samuel, the prophet. Mary groaned during worship as she poured fragrant oil onto Jesus's feet, and our Savior was anointed for burial. Regardless of whether a woman travails in prayer, worship, or giving birth, what God has spoken in heaven is now invading earth.

> God Almighty declares the word of the gospel
> with power, and the warring women of Zion
> deliver its message. (Psalm 68:11 TPT)

Yes, the Almighty has issued a divine decree for his daughter's voice to be heard like never before. *This is not a MeToo movement!* This is the Almighty's divine strategy, which is to fill his daughters with "the Seed of His Word" so that a spiritual shift is birthed in the earthly realm. What the Almighty has commissioned, he will bring it to pass.

The very heart of God is moved when he sees his children in unity and agreeing with his will, yet through travail, his daughters will birth his will on the earth. Be reminded that through this process, sonship will be revealed. We will be "the church" without spots or wrinkles. There is a major move of women coming together in great masses with the purposes of the Almighty for his children. Be encouraged for according to his Word in Jeremiah 31:15–17 AMPC):

> Thus says the LORD: A voice is heard in Ramah,
> lamentation, and bitter weeping. Rachel is weep-
> ing for her children; she refuses to be comforted
> for her children, because they are no more. Thus
> says the LORD: Restrain your voice from weep-
> ing and your eyes from tears, for your work shall
> be rewarded, says the LORD; and [your children]

shall return from the enemy's land. And there is
hope for your future, says the LORD; your children shall come back to their own country.

Children of Light

Through the blood of Jesus, we are considered "children of
Light." The Almighty Father is the "Father of Lights," and we should
not carry any form of darkness in us. Some of you are stating we are
"children of Light." We do not have any darkness in us. This statement is partially true. The blood of Jesus purified us, but we have to
maintain that purification. We have to be constantly washed with the
water of the Word, meditate on the Word, study the Word, worship,
pray, and fast with the Word.

We all battle contaminants of grumbling, complaining, unforgiveness, offense, lust of the flesh, eyes, the pride of life, and demonic
deceptions. We have to be intentional in being sanctified by God's
"truth." *Thy Word oh God is truth.* Many of us may fail to inquire of
the "Spirit of Truth" or our sweet Holy Spirit, who will lead us into
all truth.

The anointed Word of God can be likened to a savory meal for
our Spirit. *Oh, taste and see that the LORD is good (Psalm 34:8a).* Like
preparing to partake of a family meal, we would wash our hands and
then sit at the table in order to receive the meal. During these times,
there were no electronic devices (TV, phone, laptop, etc.) to distract
us. This was time to commune with one another as we partook of the
meal that was lovingly prepared for us.

In a similar manner, we are not to come into the presence of the
Holy One with various distractions. We clean our hands by lifting
them up in prayer to ask him to direct us in the Word that he desires
to release and to give us revelation of his heart concerning the Word.
Now, with expectancy, we open the Word of God, read it aloud to
build our faith, and prepare to write down what is revealed.

The Spirit of Truth delights in communing with us and will
show us the mysteries that were concealed in the Father's heart
through the Word of his Son. Partaking of the Word of God is such

an intimate experience with the Holy Spirit (who reveals the Father's heart), the Word (Jesus who declares the Father), and the Father himself, who gifted us with his son (Jesus), the Word.

The Word of God is not only "truth" but also "light" that is used to dispel all forms of darkness. *Thy word is a lamp unto my feet, and a light unto my path (Psalm 119:105 KJV).* When Jesus was led into the wilderness by the Holy Spirit, he battled Satan with the Word of God. The Apostle Paul dispels the inconsistencies of others by using the truth of the Word. Our deliverance from the darkness of grumbling, complaining, unforgiveness, offense, lust, and various demonic deceptions is by shining the light of the Word on those areas.

In this new season of shaking, the Spirit of Truth will shine the light of the Word on these dark places. This exposure will expel the darkness through repentance, seeking and releasing forgiveness, and fasting and prayerfully petitioning for the uprooting of strongholds. As we process the Word of Truth, we will be birthed into sonship and will walk as the "children of Light." *The Spirit and the bride say, "Come."*

> So, justice is driven back, and righteousness stands at a distance; truth has stumbled in the streets, honesty cannot enter. Truth is nowhere to be found, and whoever shuns evil becomes a prey. The LORD looked and was displeased that there was no justice. He saw that there was no one, he was appalled that there was no one to intervene; so, his own arm achieved salvation for him, and his own righteousness sustained him. (Isaiah 59:14–16 NIV)

CHAPTER 10

Building and Warring with the Word

> So I sent messengers to them, saying, "I am doing a great work and am unable to come down. Why should the work stop while I leave it and come down to you?" (Nehemiah 6:3 NASB)

There is a spiritual mandate for "the remnant church" *to prepare for the tsunami of souls.* Many expansion efforts have taken place before and during the start of the new decade of 2020. This is not limited to building expansions, acquiring additional property, establishing educational efforts to equip the body, or an increase in humanitarian efforts, as the list goes on.

On the devastating day of September 11, 2001, our nation was shaken by an attack from our enemy. At that time, many flocked to churches to find the answer but were introduced to religion instead of a personal relationship with Jesus. Sadly, "the church" as a whole was ill-prepared for this level of crisis. Now through rebellion against the Almighty who established the United States, we as a people have now entered into gross darkness.

Many may not realize that the United States is, in a sense, a "spiritual Israel." Israel and the United States are the only two nations whose original foundation is the Almighty God. As Israel was unprepared for a demonic attack during a holy time of rest on October 7,

2023, so the United States was at rest and unprepared on September 11. This is not a political message but a spiritual matter.

As these demonic principalities try to regain control of the world with fear, *the "sons and daughters" of the Almighty must stand in faith*. The only thing that can push back this principality of fear is by declaring the Word of God in faith through the powerful name of Jesus. *The Word of God is an eternal "seed" which produces life-bearing seeds.*

> See to it that you do not refuse him who speaks. If they did not escape when they refused him who warned them on earth, how much less will we, if we turn away from him who warns us from heaven? At that time his voice shook the earth, but now he has promised, "Once more I will shake not only the earth but also the heavens." The words "once more" indicate the removing of what can be shaken—that is, created things— so that what cannot be shaken may remain. (Hebrews 12:25–27 NIV)

In the story of Nehemiah, he was led by the Spirit to rebuild the walls of Jerusalem. Why is this important? The wall was not only a form of protection from the enemy but also functioned as a boundary. Before Nehemiah set out to rebuild the wall of Jerusalem, he fasted and prayed to the Almighty for direction and favor. Immediately, when the work began, the enemy came to ridicule the work that was being performed. The enemy tried to make *those who were called to do this great work* begin to doubt their efforts. Nehemiah had to encourage the people, and in doing so, he encouraged himself.

When the enemy realized that his words were not enough to discourage the men and women (see Nehemiah 3:12) from building, the enemy then tried intimidating them with a sneak attack. This attack was made known to Nehemiah and all those who were building. Great fear came upon those who were building with Nehemiah, but after praying to the Almighty, he encouraged the people in the LORD.

> Now when our enemies heard that it was known
> to us, and that God had frustrated their plan,
> then all of us returned to the wall, each one to his
> work. (Nehemiah 4:15 NASB)

The divine strategy was that half of the builders continued to build while the other half stood armed to fight. These warriors also stood in the places where there were still breaches in the wall, and a few had trumpets at hand to sound the alarm. The wall was quickly rebuilt, and the doors put in their place, and the gates were reinstalled. After there were no more breaches in the wall, the enemy became afraid because he knew that God had done this great work through them. The enemy ceased to try to intimidate the people with his words.

The purpose of this story in Nehemiah is to remind "the remnant church" that we are invited in this season to build with the Almighty. As we actively partner with the Almighty, we must expect demonic pushback. We have to come together on one accord and declare what the Word declares. *There is power in agreement!* The strategy of the enemy is to bring doubt about the Word of God, which is the will of God. Wherever doubt manifests, then division can take root. It's *not* time to stop building!

We are admonished by the scriptures to think on these things: *whatsoever things are true, whatsoever things are honest, whatsoever things are just, whatsoever things are pure, whatsoever things are lovely, whatsoever things are of good report; if there be any virtue, and if there be any praise, think on these things (Philippians 4:8–9 KJV).* As we allow the Holy Spirit to lead and guide us in all truth, he will reveal the plan of the enemy and give us a strategy on how to combat that plan.

We can't go any higher in God without first humbling ourselves under the mighty hand of God. The Almighty is calling us up higher in Jesus's name. The Almighty is the one who will set the pace of the building. It's our responsibility to be available and yield vessels that he can work through. Individual and corporate fasting, praying, worshipping, and meditating on God's Word are the only ways we will be able to remain in faith.

This is a time for the intercessors of God to arise and take their position on the wall. We must make sure that we have intercessors equipped to declare the Word over those vulnerable areas in the ministry. We must keep ourselves and leadership covered in prayer, stay in position, prepare to sound the alarm when necessary (as those who held the trumpets), and always be ready in season and out of season.

The Almighty is the master builder who has promised us in his Word: *He will finish the work and cut it short in righteousness: because a short work will the LORD make upon the earth (Romans 9:28 KJV).*

The imagery of building the walls of Jerusalem is a natural concept of how to spiritually build disciples of Christ Jesus. Some "ministers of the gospel" have stated that there are multiple pathways to God. Now people are looking for a path and not a person. What is written in the scripture is that *Jesus said, "I am the Way, the Truth, and the Life. No man comes to the Father except through Me" (John 4:16).* "The Way" *is a person named Jesus.*

The world does not need any man's opinion but the "*truth.*" There will be an urgency or crisis for which the Almighty is preparing "the remnant church." Jesus desires relationships, but he abhors religion. These man-made concepts (*religion*) are not the original intention of the Almighty's plan and purpose. The only acceptable religion is *"pure religion and undefiled before God and the Father is this, to visit the fatherless and widows in their affliction, and to keep himself unspotted from the world" (James 1:27 KJV).*

As stated before, we, as "the remnant church," have not been through this way before. We are co-laborers with Christ Jesus. The Father is the "master builder" who will cause the growth and increase into the believer's life. Let us beseech the LORD of harvest for more laborers, for the harvest is plentiful, but the laborers are few. Amen.

Therefore, everyone who hears these words of Mine, and acts on them, will be like a wise man who built his house on the rock. (Matthew 7:24 NASB)

CHAPTER 11

Total Surrender

> For the eyes of the LORD roam throughout the earth, so that He may strongly support those whose heart is completely His. (2 Chronicles 16:9a NASB)

The Almighty did not withhold any good thing from us (mankind) as he released his first and best love offering, who is Christ Jesus, our "kinsman-redeemer." In return, the Almighty Father expects the same level of sacrifice from his sons and daughters. The will of man is corrupt apart from the perfect will of the Almighty. However, if we relinquish our will to that of the Almighty Father in Jesus's name, he will then begin to train us on how to walk in sonship. The LORD delivered a warning rebuke, *"He will not accept a conditional surrender."* He *hates lukewarm fellowship,* and according to (Revelation 3:16), he *will vomit out of his mouth* those who choose this level of connection.

A totally surrendered heart will usher us into a level of intimacy that is beyond human reasoning or expression. The flesh is in immediate opposition to this connection because the natural part of us is in constant enmity (opposition or hostility) toward the Spirit of God. According to the Word, we are a spirit that possesses a soul and is housed in a body *(1 Thessalonians 5:23)*. In this higher level of connection, this body of flesh is buffeted by the "truth." Thy Word oh God is truth. Furthermore, we (mankind) have a solemn promise from the LORD in *(Jeremiah 24:7 NASB). I will also give them a heart to know Me, for I am the LORD; and they will be My people, and I will be their God, for they will return to Me wholeheartedly.*

Those of us who stay in position at the feet of Jesus will receive revelatory intel from his heart. The strategies of God flow freely in the secret place of the Most High, and Jesus understood this concept when he walked on the earth. The intel or revelation of what to do next was revealed when he connected to the heart of the Father. The Father and Son connected heart-to-heart or (spirit-to-spirit, and this is why he regularly stole away to be with the Father. He didn't humbly submit to the Father for the revelation that it would bring. No, Jesus desired that intimate connection with the Father. The LORD has made this intimate connection available to every son or daughter who would passionately position his or herself in the presence of the Almighty Father.

Over three years ago, the Spirit of God revealed a season of acceleration. He also warned against distractions that would hinder us from stepping into the "kairos time" or suddenly of God. He commanded that we *stay focused and remain in position.* It is not time to isolate or forsake assembling together. Soon after this warning, the demonic spirits of distraction and delay were released on the body of Christ. Through deep intercession, I heard the *Spirit of God say, "Come up higher. Yes, come up higher so that you can see with clarity and hear without hindrances."* Now many in the body of Christ are dealing with this demonic spirit of delay and distraction that was sent from the pits of hell to wear out the saints. *But God!* The Almighty has declared, "No more delay!" The Spirit of God is calling us "the remnant church" higher in him.

The LORD God sees the end from the beginning. Jesus did not come into the world in vain and then to allow the enemy to wreak havoc on his "church." Jesus promised, and he can't lie…that *the gates of hell will not prevail against his "church."* This is *not* the time for "the church" to get their rapture rugs ready! We are dealing with spiritual warfare. This is not the time to shrink back and cower in fear because of the darkness that we see.

The Lion of Judah is roaring over his church to wake us from slumber. The Father of Lights will train our hands to war in this time. He is exposing the darkness in order to expel it, which will give us revelation on how to take back territory and how to further his kingdom in the earthly realm. Through the Word of God, we, "the church," will be trained on how to war from our positions in the heavenly places.

> Proclaim this among the nations: "Prepare for war! Wake up the mighty men, let all the men of war draw near, let them come up." (Joel 3:9 NKJV)

We are the generation that the LORD God has entrusted with his glorious might to push back the realm of darkness, reclaim territory, do great exploits, and further the kingdom of God in the earthly realm. The Almighty proclaimed, "Eye has not seen, ear has not heard, nor has it come into the heart of man what things God has prepared for those who love him" (1 Corinthians 2:9).

There is a demonic storm coming, yet it is already here. This is likened to the time when a great storm was on the sea, and the "Prince of Peace" (Jesus) came walking on the water. The storm was still raging when Jesus bid Peter to come to him on the water. Peter's focus on Jesus kept him in faith, but once the wind distracted him, then fear gripped him to the point that he sank. We, like Peter, have to keep our eyes of faith in Jesus, who causes us to walk on what is trying to take us under.

The evil one is counting on "the church" to get into fear so that he can get the upper hand. The enemy uses the same tactics over and over again. Once the evil one successfully wears down the saints of God, then he releases the *spirit of fear. But God!* The Almighty commands us to *fear not!* The remnant church came into agreement, declared the Word of God in faith, and sealed it with the powerful name of Jesus. This time, the *LORD of Host* will give strategies before the attack to frustrate the plans of the evil one. Likened to the days of Elisha when the Syrian king came against the king of Israel in 2 KINGS 6:8–10 (CEV).

> Time after time, when the king of Syria was at war against the Israelites, he met with his officers and announced, "I've decided where we will set up camp." Each time, Elisha would send this warning to the king of Israel: "Don't go near there. That's where the Syrian troops have set up camp." So the king would warn the Israelite troops in that place to be on guard.

Guidance of the Holy Spirit

First of all, the Holy Spirit is the third person of the Godhead. All believers are sealed in Jesus with the Holy Spirit of promise, which is given as a pledge of inheritance from the Almighty Father (see Ephesians 1:13b–14). After Jesus's resurrection, he breathed on the disciples and said, "Receive the Holy Spirit" (John 20:22). The spirit that was on Jesus was imparted to his disciples, like new believers in Jesus who receive the fullness of the same spirit. In obedience to Jesus, 120 persons (male and female) were united in faith, and the upper room was suddenly filled, endowed, and immersed in the Dunamis power of the Holy Spirit (see Acts 2:1–6). This immersion of power enables every believer who is humbly submitted to the Holy Spirit to do his acts: signs, wonders, and miracles to flow through the believer's life. Apart from the Holy Spirit, who is God, we can do nothing. The Spirit of Truth will give revelation to the Word, unify the body of Christ (the church), pray groanings that cannot be uttered in perfect alignment with the Almighty's will, and teach us how to use spiritual weapons. The demonic storm that has already been released cannot be fought through the flesh but through the Spirit.

> For though we walk in the flesh, we do not war after the flesh: For the weapons of our warfare

> are not carnal, but mighty through God to the pulling down of strongholds. Casting down imaginations, and every high thing that exalted itself against the knowledge of God and bringing into captivity every thought to the obedience of Christ. (2 Corinthians 10:3–5 KJV)

Sadly, "the church" is weak and sick because the Holy Spirit has not been totally yielded to. Yes, the Spirit of Truth can be grieved, but he will never leave us nor forsake us. We have been warned *not to quench the Holy Spirit* (1 Thessalonians 5:19). Because of the zealous love of the Spirit of Truth for the body of Christ, he will bring great conviction so that "the remnant church" will be led into the holiness of God.

The Spirit of God knows the heart of the Almighty and endows the believer with the will of the Father. Many do not realize that "the remnant church" is the one who is ordained to continue the book of Acts. The book of Acts is simply a few documented accounts of the workings of the Holy Spirit. Nothing has been documented of the greater works that will be done through the total surrender to the Holy Spirit. Jesus does give us a clue of what a total surrender to the Spirit will produce.

> I assure you, most solemnly I tell you, if anyone steadfastly believes in Me, he will himself be able to do the things that I do; and he will do even greater things than these, because I go to the Father. (John 14:12 AMPC)

CHAPTER 12

The Sound of Unity

> I do not pray for these alone, but also for those
> who will believe in Me through their word; that
> they all may be one, as You, Father, are in Me,
> and I in You; that they also may be one in Us,
> that the world may believe that You sent Me.
> (John 17:20–21)

There is a sound that can pierce through the heavens and gain the attention of the Almighty. In the days of Nimrod, it was a unified sound of rebellion. The LORD God descended from heaven to make a righteous judgment against the sound that was released. Perceiving the wickedness of their hearts, the LORD confused their language and scattered them throughout the world.

Throughout Jesus's earthly ministry, he had men and women who were his disciples. Jesus paid for the penalty of mankind's sin through his death and redeemed us through his precious blood. *When Jesus died on the cross, his side was pierced to reestablish the woman's position of authority that she held in the beginning.*

What does this have to do with the sound of unity? *Everything! It is God's original intention that we (men and women) unite as one as it was in the beginning.*

Before Jesus ascended back to the Father, *he appeared to more than five hundred of the brothers and sisters at the same time, most of whom are still living, though some have fallen asleep (1 Corinthians 15:6 NIV).* They all were instructed to tarry in Jerusalem until they were endowed with power from on high. In *Acts 1:12–14*, we see that men and women were gathered together in obedient alignment with Jesus's command.

All these were continually devoting themselves with one mind to prayer, along with the women, and Mary, the mother of Jesus, and with His brothers (Acts 1:14 NASB). When the day of Pentecost had fully come, these ones were united as one. The sound of unity pierced the darkness and filled the throne room of the Living God.

The Holy Spirit was so moved by the sound that his entrance was recorded as a mighty rushing wind. The unity that was present in the birthing of the church was based on the fundamental doctrine of the kingdom of God, which was taught to them by Jesus. We see throughout the conception of the early church that the apostles had different views but always referred back to the fundamental basics of Christ Jesus's teaching.

A prime example of this is when a centurion named Cornelius had a visit from an angel who instructed him to send for Simon, who is called Peter. Because of the tender mercies of the LORD, he continued to give revelation to the apostles. Peter fell into a trance and saw a sheet lowered with unclean animals on it. *A voice came to him, "Get up, Peter, kill and eat!" But Peter said, "By no means, LORD, for I have never eaten anything unholy and unclean." Again, a voice came to him a second time, "What God has cleansed, no longer consider unholy"* (Acts 10:13–15 NASB). Three times, he was commanded to kill and eat, but being Jewish, this seemed to be contrary to the law of Moses. Revelation was imparted to Peter concerning the LORD's will to go with the Gentiles who were waiting on him.

The Jews were under Roman control, and thus, they had no dealings with one another. After Peter ministered to Cornelius, his family, and friends were all filled with the Holy Spirit during the message. The other apostles heard of this and questioned Peter and the brethren who accompanied him. Peter shared the heavenly revelation, and all the brothers rejoiced in the LORD greatly. The apostles remembered what the prophet Isaiah spoke about Christ.

> Here is my servant, whom I uphold, my chosen
> one in whom I delight; I will put my Spirit on
> him, and he will bring justice to the nations.
> (Isaiah 42:1 AMPC)

The point that is being made is that revelation given by the Spirit of Truth will never contradict the Word. Instead of fighting or debating about what should have happened, the apostles *yielded to the will of God.* This is key in order to remain in accord with the spirit of the Living God. Man's opinions do not matter, but the revelation of "truth" according to the Spirit of Truth will cause unity to be maintained. *Carry each other's burdens, and in this way, you will fulfill the law of Christ (Galatians 6:2 NIV).*

There are "giants" in the land!

From the giving of "the law" that defined sin to the fulfillment of the law under the "new covenant" through the blood of Christ Jesus, there has been a spirit of deception from the evil one to cause division. This division has been so subtle in keeping many from uniting as one. However, war of a common enemy, in many cases, has a way of breaking down the lines that divide. For centuries, the church has been divided on matters that are not aligned with the basic fundamental teachings of Jesus.

While many in the body of Christ have been preoccupied with a difference of opinions in the matters of the doctrines of men, the "giants" have crept in unnoticed by many. In just one generation or forty years, the morals of people, the influence of the gospel of Christ, the honor of the aged, and those in positions of authority have been lost to rebellion.

A "holy war" has been declared by the LORD of Host, and it will shake the very foundations of the "seven mountains of influence." The seven mountains of influence are as follows: (1) religion, (2) family, (3) education, (4) business, (5) media, (6) government, and (7) arts and entertainment. The Holy Spirit is declaring the same anointed words that David was given before battling Goliath. *And David said, "What have I now done? Is there not a cause?" (1 Samuel 17:29 KJV).*

Is there not a cause? Yes, there is an eternal covenant. The new covenant that was inaugurated by the precious shed blood of Jesus is the confidence that we stand on and the cause that we fight for. Like David, who went up against Goliath with a sling and rock because he had a revelation about who his God is. This same revelation of who Jesus truly is is the foundation of "the church." We will war as David did from the place of revelation, and it will cause the enemy to scatter in fear by the powerful name of Jesus.

> He said to them, "But who do you say that I am?" Simon Peter answered and said, "You are the Christ, the Son of the living God." Jesus answered and said to him, "Blessed are you, Simon Bar-Jonah, for flesh and blood has not revealed this to you, but My Father who is in heaven. And I also say to you that you are Peter, and on this rock I will build My church, and the gates of Hades shall not prevail against it. And I will give you the keys of the kingdom of heaven, and whatever you bind on earth be bound in heaven, and whatever you loose on earth will be loosed in heaven." (Matthew 16:15–19 KJV)

The earth is the LORD's and all that it contains. These seven mountains of influence currently have "giants" occupying them. However, the shaking of created things is starting to bring to light what was hidden in the dark. The Father of Lights will position his "children of Light" on these "seven mountains of influence" so that we are empowered to further his kingdom by using the keys that have been given to the church. Through the Spirit of the Living God, he is uniting the body of Christ to minister to lost souls. It's not the Father's will that any perish, but all come to repentance with the full knowledge of Christ Jesus. The Gospel of Jesus will spread quickly because of the spiritual hunger of the people. We must be ready! *Jesus is coming quickly!*

We have come to share in Christ if, indeed, we hold our original conviction firmly to the very end. *As has just been said: "Today, if you hear his voice, do not harden your hearts as you did in the rebellion. Who were they who heard and rebelled? Were they not all those Moses led out of Egypt? And with whom was he angry for forty years? Was it not with those who sinned, whose bodies perished in the wilderness?" (Hebrew 3:14–17 NIV).*

PRAYER OF SALVATION

Jesus, forgive me for everything that I have done wrong. I invite you into my life, and I know you can make me new through your love. I accept you to be the LORD of my life to guide me in everything I do. Thank you, Jesus, for saving my life as my Savior and guiding me as my LORD. I welcome your Holy Spirit to fill me with the power to be strengthened in the way that you have me go. In Jesus's name, Amen.

Katherine D. Walker is a tenacious pursuer of the heart of God who willingly stands in the gap as an intercessor. Her greatest desire is to see all nations burning with the zealous desire to connect with Jesus in a loving and intimate relationship. Through this relationship with Jesus, many will accept the charge to operate as the sons and daughters of the Most High God. She is a prophetic evangelist who has done and will continue to do many good things to further the kingdom of God. She and her family reside in Chattanooga, Tennessee.

www.ingramcontent.com/pod-product-compliance
Lightning Source LLC
Chambersburg PA
CBHW020328180726
47991CB00019B/1066